Commercial Real Estate

Commercial real estate Guide for Beginners

Samuel Gobar

☐ Copyright 2016 by Samuel Gobar - All rights reserved.

-

The following eBook is reproduced below with the goal of providing information that is as accurate and reliable as possible. Regardless, purchasing this eBook can be seen as consent to the fact that both the publisher and the author of this book are in no way experts on the topics discussed within, and that any recommendations or suggestions that are made herein are for entertainment purposes only. Professionals should be consulted as needed prior to undertaking any of the action endorsed herein.

This declaration is deemed fair and valid by both the American Bar Association and the Committee of Publishers Association and is legally binding throughout the United States.

Furthermore, the transmission, duplication or reproduction of any of the following work including specific information will be considered an illegal act, irrespective of if it is done electronically or in print. This extends to creating a secondary or tertiary copy of the work or a recorded copy; and this is only allowed with express written consent from the Publisher. All additional right reserved.

The information in the following pages is broadly considered to be a truthful and accurate account of facts and as such; any inattention, use or misuse of the information in question by the reader will render any resulting actions solely under their purview. There are no scenarios in which the publisher or the original author of this work can be in any fashion deemed liable for any hardship or damages that may befall them after undertaking information described herein.

Additionally, the information in the following pages is intended only for informational purposes and should thus be thought of as universal. As befitting its nature, it is presented without assurance regarding its prolonged validity or interim quality. Trademarks that are mentioned are done without written consent and can in no way be considered an endorsement from the trademark holder.

Introduction

The following chapters will discuss the different advantages and positive aspects of commercial real estate.

You will discover how important it is to always make the right investments in commercial property.

The final chapter will give you the information that you need on the specific terms that are common in commercial buildings.

There are plenty of books on this subject on the market, thanks again for choosing this one! Every effort was made to ensure it is full of as much useful information as possible. Please enjoy!

Table of Contents

Introduction 4

Chapter 1: An Overview of Commercial Real Estate 1

Chapter 2: Generating Leads on Commercial Properties 4

Chapter 3: Determine the Value of a Property 8

Chapter 4: The Right Financing for Your Properties 12

Chapter 5: Understanding the Way that You Can Make Money 16

Chapter 6: Profiting from Management of Your Time 19

Chapter 7: Managing Your Properties the Right Way 25

Chapter 8: What is a Good Deal on a Commercial Property? ... 30

Chapter 9: Mortgage Options You Have 38

Chapter 10: Problems that Commercial Property Owners Face 42

Chapter 11: How to Get the Best Deal on Commercial Property Financing 47

Chapter 12: The Plan for Your Property Investment Business .. 51

Chapter 13: Terms that You Will Find in Commercial Real Estate 56

Chapter 14: The Right Commercial Property for You 60

Conclusion 70

Chapter 1: An Overview of Commercial Real Estate

Understanding the difference in commercial real estate and residential real estate investing is as simple as knowing the difference in a home that people live in and a business that people work in. When you are figuring out how to make money with commercial real estate, you need to find out what is going to be popular in your area. For example, if you live in a large city, it will be better to have office buildings as commercial real estate. If you reside in a small town or even in an area where there is a lot of factory work and production, you may be better purchasing and renting out things like where businesses are located. The commercial real estate that will be profitable will be dependent on the area that you are in — nearly every location is going to be different.

It is a good idea to learn about commercial real estate before you jump into it. You need to know what is selling, what is not renting out and what is going to work best for you. You should also know the specifics of commercial real estate in your area. Are there laws that govern what you can and can't rent out? Do you have to follow certain codes? Is there a limit to how many commercial buildings you own before you become a principal developer? All of these questions are ones that can't be answered by this book but will instead need to be figured out in a more local sense.

By reading this book, you will be able to figure out what type of property will be profitable for you, the amount that particular properties are worth and the best ways to finance the property. You can also learn the negotiation tactics that pros use so that you can try to make the most out of the process. It is a good idea always to figure out how you can benefit from the tax breaks and the deals that are sometimes found with commercial properties. Try your best, and you will be able to have the best experience possible with commercial real estate.

Having commercial real estate can be a hugely lucrative investment. Not only is it a career that you can benefit from in the *now*, but it is also something that will bring in residual income for years to come. When you find the right type of property and the right way to market it, there is very little work that you will have to do later on. It will give you the chance to continue to collect money for a period in the future – you'll be able to benefit from the work that you put into it.

Commercial real estate investment, while lucrative, can be a huge time and money investment. You will need to put a lot of work and capital into your commercial real estate so be sure that you are prepared for that. It is a good idea always to try and make sure that you are prepared as much as possible for the things that are going to come in the future. Always do your best and make sure that you are getting money built up and money that you can put aside to be able to contribute to your real estate investment.

Chapter 2: Generating Leads on Commercial Properties

Knowing the right type of commercial property to invest in is only half of the process. Once you figure out what is going to work for you and what is going to make the most money, you need to work to make sure that you can find that property. To generate leads on properties that you can purchase and then turn around and rent out, you will need to take a few steps. These are important in that you can find the exact property that is perfect for you. They don't have to be followed in order; so try out different things until you find that perfect system that works for you.

A Lookout

You may consider hiring someone who can find the perfect commercial property for you. This is a bird dog or a lookout. They are trained to be able to find the best properties, and they will make the best decision possible for you. They can give you a list of properties and then you can make a choice from there on what you want to be able to purchase.

One thing that you should always do is hire a lookout who is a professional. With these professionals, you can give them a list of what you want in a property. They will then be able to look at the different things that you want and come back with a list of commercial real estates that is going to work for you.

This should be one of the last resorts for you. You will have to pay for this, and it will often be costly, so try to make sure that you can find something on your own first.

Land Developers

For many real estate investors, the end game is to become a land developer. This is where the real money is. While you are waiting at that point and just getting started, you can take advantage of these developers. It is a good idea to become friendly with developers. They are looking for people just like you – those who want to buy commercial properties. When you work with a developer, you will be sure that you are getting the best chance possible at the various options included in real estate investment for commercial properties.

The best thing about working with a developer is that they can often offer you deals that typical agents would not be able to offer you. Since they are the ones who developed the property, they will be in a better position to take money off of the bottom line so that you can get the best price possible.

Always make sure that, if you are working with a developer, it is someone who is reputable. You will be able to make more money and get a better deal if you work with someone who has a good reputation.

Simple Looking

Just driving around and looking at commercial properties for sale can be the best way to find a property. This is especially true in small towns and rural areas where there is not a lot of square mileage to drive around. You should make sure that you are looking at *all* of your options when you are looking around so that you can find out the different things that are included with the properties.

As you are looking around, be sure to figure out what the property entails – what is the cost of it, what do you think it is worth and where is it located? These questions will help you to make a decision later on; so, you may want to write down the answers for each of them according to the properties that you are looking at.

Take your time when you are looking. The first time that you are looking – just do that. Later on, you can contact real estate agents and try to find out more about the property. There are many steps to this process; so, be sure that you follow them.

Network with Others

There are many real estate networks available to investors even if you are in a small town with not a lot of major options. It is a good idea to always network with other people so that you can make the best choice possible. If you have a friend with a commercial property for sale, they will be more likely to sell to you than they would be to a random person; so, try to make business friends with everyone that you meet in the industry.

Networking is a great way to get a good start. Not only will it help you to figure out what type of property is going to work the best for you and also help to find that property, but it will also help you make contacts in other areas of real estate. From agents to inspectors and everything in between, a strong network is imperative to making a lot of money.

Try a Different Approach

Nearly all investors are doing the same things and trying the same tactics. If you want to be different, try something different. That could mean that you buy low-value properties and switch them up. It could also mean that you try to find properties that are in different areas. No matter what you are doing, you need to make sure that you are going to be able to figure out the right way to be able to get the best experience possible. It is also a wise decision to try and make sure that you are finding the best properties. There is a large profit margin that can come from finding the right property. When you are able to find that profit margin and are able to make it work for your investments, you will be able to get a much higher profit. It is something that real estate investors have been using for a long time and something that you can also benefit from in your investment business.

Chapter 3: Determine the Value of a Property

To be able to make money from your commercial real estate investments, you will need to know the value of the property. The value takes everything into consideration – from the actual property worth to the amount that you can expect to bring in from the property over the years. There are many different things that you should take into consideration, and each of these will allow you to adjust the worth of the property. It is a good idea to know the value so that you can set the price to what you want to be able to do.

The Age of the Property

In some instances, newer properties will be worth more because of the options that they come with. In other instances, where buildings are better because they are vintage, older properties will be worth more. The age of the property will nearly always be taken into account when you look at the property; so, be sure that you are working to find out what is going to work for you.

Appraisal Value of It

You should always have the property professionally appraised. This is something that will show you what the true value of the property is. If you can do this before you buy the property, you will have a better chance of making more money off of it since you will know what the value of it is. If you do not do this before, it is important that you do it almost immediately after you have made the decision to purchase the property to rent out to others.

How Large It Is

The size of the space will determine how much money you should pay for it and how much money you will be able to get for it. Obviously, the larger the building is, the more expensive it will be for you to try and purchase. There are many instances when you might not need that space, though, so make sure that is something you are prepared for. You should always figure out how space is going to work for you and whether it will come in handy when you are renting the property out to other people for business use.

The Demand for Property like It

There will be a different amount of demand for different properties depending on the area that you are in. For example, some properties will cost much more in different areas because of the way that the properties are set up. It is a good idea to make sure that you are getting what you can out of the properties so that you know what the demand for each of the properties is in your area. It is a wise decision to be able to help people figure out what they are looking for and what they can do with various property options.

What It Can Be Used For

If you buy an office building, it will only be able to be used for offices. If you buy a warehouse, the same thing applies. You need to make sure that you are doing what you can to provide a building that is able to be used for different purposes. The more purposes a building has when it comes to your various options, the better chance you will have at making sure that the value is as high as possible. It is a good decision to choose a multipurpose building over one that only has a singular purpose.

The Zoning on It

Depending on where you live, there will be requirements on the zoning of your property. A property that is zoned in one way will not be able to be used for anything other than what it is zoned for. If you find a property that is not zoned for more than one thing, it may be a good idea to stay away from it. Zoning will depend on what the property can do, the area it is located and what you can put into it so that you can make sure that you are getting the best experience possible. Zone the property in a way that makes sense and the value will be changed.

Your Ability to Profit

The value of the property can change depending on how much you can profit from it as a rental. It is a good idea to try your best to figure out exactly what you are going to get from it on a monthly basis, a yearly basis and with a 5-year outlook on the property. You need to make sure that you are doing many different things with your property so be sure that you look at all of the aspects that will allow you to make the most amount of profit possible.

The Expected Life of the Property

There will come a time when you are no longer able to rent the property out. This is when the life of the property is over. It most commonly happens when the building gets old, when you are not able to make profits from it and when major things start happening to the property to decrease the value. Figure out when that point is and then calculate from when you are purchasing it until then. This is the expected life of the property, and it will make a difference with the way that you can rent it out. Be sure that you know this; and that will help to tell you the value.

Expected Value after Improvements

You should consider some of the improvements that you are going to make on the property. While you don't necessarily have to do a full flip on it or renovate it in the best way possible, you should consider the small improvements that you are going to make. From there, figure out what the value will be with the improvements that you are going to do to it. This will help you to understand the way that the property works.

Chapter 4: The Right Financing for Your Properties

Using Cash for the Investment

Cash is your best option to ensure that you don't start your business out in the opening, which is the only path that you'll ever have to start out profiting from your real estate investments once you start the business enterprise. It is smart to always try to be sure that you will be using cash every time that you do ventures. Few people, though, can to begin spending with cash. If you'd like to start out with the money option, you will need to be sure that you make an effort and conserve so as to start investing straight away (unless, of course, you've received an inheritance or another lump amount of cash).

Start by conserving a tiny amount and build up to where you desire to be. If you're currently working, reserve 5% of your salary for saving. When you are more comfortable with that, reserve 7% and finally build up until you have the total amount that you'll require to have the ability to acquire an investment property.

If you're going to acquire one, you will likely just need to conserve for the first one. Be sure you save the total amount of the business and any work that you should do for the business to enable you to ensure that you have lots of money left so that you have the ability to focus on it. Once you've purchased one investment property, you can sell it for income, turn around and purchase another one with the money you made and set some money aside every time you do it so that you will eventually have a nice stack of profit. This is the way that you can turn a profit. If you're purchasing a property as accommodations, you can certainly do a similar thing, just don't sell the business which you have - instead, lease it out to people and use the amount of money that originates from that as your earnings.

With Credit

This is actually the most popular option as it pertains to investing in commercial properties. Although it might not exactly be the least expensive option because you will wrap up repaying interest rates, it is exactly what most folks have to do because they just don't possess thousands of dollars sitting down in their bank-account. There are many steps that you'll require to take to make certain which you can use credit to get:

- Pay down the personal types of debt - if you have a home loan it yourself, try your hardest to have the ability to pay it back

- Have a better looking credit history - you may use various solutions to raise your credit history, but it will always be smart to try to make certain that your credit score is right and that you can get a small business loan

-       Conversation with your standard bank - set up a good romantic relationship with your lender and ensure that you tell them that you want to eventually have a loan out with them to enable you to start your real business investing

-       Minimize spending - avoid your bank cards or revolving lending options if you don't have to, so as to use the amount of money to get more and to enable you to ensure that you aren't needing to spend big money by paying credit card debt

-       Save money - in case you will use credit to have the ability to choose the property, you should still make an effort to save money

When You Don't Have Cash or Credit

The most frequent situation for not doing real estate investment when someone would like to is the fact they don't have the funds or the credit to have the ability to do it. You might be amazed to find you don't need either of these to get started on real estate trading. All you need is to have the capability to be crafty, and you'll be able to start out buying properties. Try one of these options:

OPM - other's money. That's where you acquire from a member of family or a pal. Be careful if you are doing this since it can create stress and dissolve friendships. Make sure that you are obvious on the conditions of the loan, with both parties knowing what they want from it. Consider pulling up an agreement together.

Crowdsourcing - that's where many people provide you with the money to cover the property. This is a tricky action to take; ensure that you write down reasonable explanation for attempting to undertake it. Be genuine about the amount of money that you will be boosting and let people know your true known reasons for wanting to get it done (even if it is merely to produce a lot of cash).

Angel lending options - these kind of loans do not come from anywhere else apart from a normal lender. They will be the way that you can earn a living from individuals who are wealthy and want to provide away their money or who wish to give you a hand. These loans are excellent – however, they will often have high-interest rates.

Your premises - if you have your premises, you can get started flipping it to market or book. A lot of folks who don't possess money to buy a fresh property will just use their own and then go from the gains that they make from it.

Chapter 5: Understanding the Way that You Can Make Money

The less overall you need to spend on the business and the next flip of the business, the more income you'll be able to make. If you're in a position to get much on the amount of money that you put in, you can boost your profit margin which allows you the opportunity to make even more income from the properties that you have, and that you get in the foreseeable future. It is smart to always save just as much money since you can also make an effort to get discounts on both genuine property and the structure area of the flipping process.

Materials

The materials that you utilize for your investment property can start to have a toll on your finances. Finding much on labor and on materials is nearly as important as finding much over a home that you will be going to turn. The materials that you utilize should be high-quality; nonetheless, they also need to not trim very far into the budget. Ensure that you find materials and labor that straddle the fine collection between being inexpensive and being truly a surprisingly high quality which could appear expensive to potential buyers.

If you anticipate getting into the business investment business, it may be beneficial to form an operating marriage with a wholesaler. You might desire a business license or perhaps a membership cost to enable you get materials at a general price. However, the charge will more often than not be worth the amount of money that you save, particularly if you've planned on flipping a whole lot of properties. Just ensure that you will work with an established wholesaler who's going to market your items which are damaged, taken or otherwise affected. Buying at low cost can also void the warrantee that is included with these articles.

It is worth looking into clearance materials. Ensure that they may be on clearance for no reason apart from them simply not selling. They shouldn't be damaged. Some clearance items do not sell because they're an unpopular color or style, you can find lucky and discover extremely popular materials that were just purchased in excess. If you're considering buying materials on clearance, always find out why, exactly why it is on clearance. Additionally, it is a good notion to determine if buying it on clearance could void the warranty on that.

Other ways that you can spend less is to buy products at a low price. High-quality products that are established at regular price can save money if you get the merchandise that will be the midsection of the series. You don't need the most notable of the range because they'll not pay off in the long run, and may end up looking ubiquitous in a home that you will be selling. Additionally, you don't want anything from underneath of the collection; because the materials tend to be cheap and may compromise the grade of the home.

While they aren't the central part of your flip and can certainly consume your entire budget, there are things that you need to consider as it pertains to your materials. Materials will most likely not be the priciest part of your flip, and actually should be treated as such: materials. Ensure that you purchase ones that your service provider could work with, which you feel more comfortable with advertising to your audience. Save nearly all your restoration budget to pay the company who'll be the priciest aspect of the flip apart from purchasing the home.

Chapter 6: Profiting from Management of Your Time

If you are doing any project, it will always be smart to do your very best to manage your time and effort so you can get the most from the time that you may spend on a job. Factors to consider whenever you are flipping residences or focusing on investment properties; is that you take care of your time and effort as wisely as possible. This will help you become more successful with your own time and may also enable you to boost your profit percentage on the businesses that you will be flipping.

Focus on Big Assignments First

Among the first rules of your time management is to take on the daunting duties first, so the smaller responsibilities will feel small in comparison. When you ensure that you focus on the best business jobs first, you'll be able to become more prepared for little things. Bonus offer: a few of little things could get done when you are focusing on bigger assignments and making them your priority.

When you have something like plumbing related or electrical that should be attended to, have your companies do this work first. This will likely be one of the primary elements of the project and can probably need you to tear down surfaces within the home. If you focus on these first, you can avoid needing to tear down surfaces which you have painted or installed new cabinets. By doing these big things first, you can make sure that you don't need to backtrack on the task that you do, or have to totally redo it because you had to rip walls down.

While it could be tempting since it can make an enormous difference in a home, don't ever focus on the painting. The coloring on your home ought to be the very last thing that is done, and should be achieved by contracted painters. Even though you are at the end of assembling your project, you don't know if you will need to pull a wall socket out of any wall membrane or make alterations on a wall structure that was just coated. By making the painting job the very last thing that you do, you will put away from yourself some grief at the end of the job.

Set a period Limit

Each portion of the home must have a period limit onto it. Your contractor will most likely set a period limit for his target job to be achieved in each section of the home, but retain in mind that they can probably review that point limit.

By setting your time and effort limit, you'll be able to prepare yourself when each goes independently. Consider adding around 10% of the time period they have set for a task to be achieved. For instance, if your company says a project will be achieved in 10 days and nights, add a supplementary day; so you will not be sorely disappointed when each goes over.

The greater businesses you spend money on, the much more likely you'll be able to learn whether a period limit is likely to be realistic. Talk to your service provider before they start the business, and get their notion of what the amount of time the work will need. They have the best idea because they're accustomed to carrying out work like that, plus they understand how long it requires each of the subcontractors to have the ability to do the task for them.

If things don't get done in a degree of time, press your service provider to get his crews to work better. There's always work that you can do. Your general builder should be working as hard as is feasible to accomplish this as fast as possible. So long as you have let her or him know that you will be trying to turn the business, they ought to know that your earnings (and their repayment) will depend on how quickly they can get things done. A period limit can help them to learn they are under great pressure to get things done as fast as possible.

Generate a Contingency Time Budget

You might have a contingency cover your finances; why not need one for enough time that will be allocated to the job? Adding expected perfect time to the project can make an overdue job less of a blow on the strain that you'll already have encompassing the business and the flipping process. When you have a contingency set up for a while, you'll be able to make use of that up whenever your contractors inform you they are not heading to get things done as quickly as you had anticipated.

The contingency time budget is something that will continue to work wonders for the strain that you are feeling if you are in flipping businesses. Your companies might not exactly have considered a few extra times in, but you would have. They'll continue steadily to work hard, but you'll possess the satisfaction of understanding that you should have more time if something will go wrong.

Among the easiest techniques that you can do is to program your open up business around fourteen days after your contractor's expected end day. If the task is performed before, simply move your open up business up which is a lot easier than endeavoring to push it back again.

USE Contractors

You don't automatically have to get smart with the companies who will work on your home, but do anything that you can to help them out with the job. If indeed they need permits, provide them with the information that they need to take to the town. If indeed they need paperwork from you, make it important. Your contractor is working as quickly as is feasible, which means that your project is certain to get done as fast as possible. Don't make their job harder.

If there are small things that can be done to help the builder; like transporting in resources for painters, or assisting to screw on electric outlet plates, get it done. You might be paying for everything as it pertains to the restoration, but there is certainly nothing stating that you can't help. Keep in mind, the more assistance the contractors do get, the faster the job will be completed. If assembling your project gets done before your planned date, you'll be able to make more income on it; plus much more quickly than what you have attempted to do.

Chapter 7: Managing Your Properties the Right Way

Finding the property and financing it is only half of the challenges that you must overcome in venturing into real estate business. It is a good idea to make sure that you are working to provide the people who you are renting to the opportunity to have a lasting business solution. When you are managing the property that you are renting out to businesses, it is important that you always try to make sure that you are doing it the right way. There are certain things that will make your job easier and others that will make your job harder. Make sure that you know what each of these is and try to give yourself the opportunity to be the best commercial property manager.

An Appropriate Price

Pricing your premises for the right amount could be the difference in an effective property management and losing profits because you didn't deal with it correctly. You should ensure that you charge your property in line with the value and the area that you will be in. If you're unable to do this, then there's a chance that you'll not have the ability to maximize the sum of money possible. You should try to make certain that your premises are certainly going for the right price - whether that is 80 us dollars monthly or 800 us dollars per month.

Ensuring the Right Tenants

Tenants can make an enormous difference in the sort of property to have and you ought to ensure that you're getting the right kind of tenant. Doing things such as learning about their record, adding information about them and creating various things for them allows you to ensure that you will be going to have the ability to hold the best experience possible. Your tenants will be better suitable for your premises if you ensure that they have got the income to have the ability to shell out the dough.

Don't Get Too Close

It may seem to be like a good notion to be friendly with your tenants, but don't get too close to them. When people feel that their property administrator is their good friend, they'll not want to pay their charges on time. That is true generally, and you ought to ensure that you do what you can to permit yourself to hold the best experience possible. It is smart to just be their business director - don't make an effort to make tenants friends.

Offer Incentives

Although, it is not unusual for folks to simply stop paying their lease bill; there are things that can be done to make people want to pay their rent even more. Which means that you'll need to consider offering bonuses to them. Make an effort to make sure that you will be going to permit people the opportunity to truly generate profits, and that they can find the best experience possible. Apart from being able to continue operating their business in the specified space, you can offer things that will always make them want to pay their rent.

Collect a Deposit from the Tenants

Always get a first deposit on the business. This can stop people from thinking about putting openings in the wall membrane or ruining your carpet. The first deposit should add up to per month of hire and can get when the rent is up if the business is in good shape. Tell them that they can be capable of getting their deposit back again only if the exact property is strictly how it was when you initially rented it out to them.

Be Careful with the Business

There are some businesses that you may simply not want to rent to. There are some businesses that are protected under laws, but there are others that you need to just avoid at all costs. It is a good idea to never rent out your building to massage parlors, tattoo businesses or certain types of businesses that are seedy. It is hard to verify the legality of each of these, and with the problems running rampant in each of these locations; the problems may fall back on you.

Choose Buildings that Are Nice

Factors to consider to making your space as nice as it can be so as to lease it out to the right people. There are numerous people who'll simply want to hire your business since it appears as nice as it can be. There are many choices that you'll make to make certain that your premises is nice. Make sure that you are employing these in your favor and make sure that you're getting the best experience possible. Always make an effort to make your space nice and make it a good space that folks would want to reside in.

Act as a Good Landlord Manager

It's important that your tenants have a landlord they know they can count on. This isn't to state that you ought to be their best good friend, but that you ought to be providing them with a safe location to live. When something needs set, take action. When someone needs help, help them. Even though you will work as a landlord rather than as a pal, you ought to be able to make certain that you will be assisting people when they would like to be helped.

Know When to Ask for Help

You may sometimes need help as it pertains to the business that you've got. Whether which means that you employ the service of a manager by yourself, a maintenance person or even legal help when you have problematic tenants, there are specific things that can be done to ensure that you will be getting the assistance that you'll require. Don't be worried to ask visitors to help you, especially pros. It will always be smart to find the help that you'll require and ensure that you do anything that you can to make your premises the best that it could be.

Chapter 8: What is a Good Deal on a Commercial Property?

If you are first starting out, it may seem to be easy to feel that you're getting a good deal over a home because it has a minimal price. But, buyers beware. A minimal price on the home could sign problems, and you will need to ensure that you will be truly obtaining a package before you decide to flip the business. Make sure to take each one of these things into consideration before you get the home. The greater that you turn businesses as assets, the easier it'll be that you can determine whether something is a package or not.

Costs Associated with Business

The expense of the business is the bottom price that you will be looking at the business for. This is exactly what the business is stated at and what you will probably pay for the business if you are paying in cash.

There could be other activities that are from home, such as shutting costs. This can be put into the expense of the home if you are figuring it out about a budget and then for determining if you're getting a package or not.

Ensure that you know the price tag on other businesses in the region. If the business is related to those, this can be a great buy for you. If it's far below the worthiness of other businesses in the region, retreat! It might be so low because there are issues with it. By looking at other comparative businesses in the region, you'll have a good notion of what you ought to be paying. So long as the home doesn't have many more rooms or is a totally different design as the other businesses, you should pay just across the same amount as how many other businesses are.

If you are looking at the price tag on the business, only consider the genuine cost of the business. It might be useful that you can make a spreadsheet or a graph that you can complete if you are taking a look at businesses that can potentially, become the next flip. Complete the expense of the business in the region to have set aside with the budget. You can create another brand for the home loan and the next interest obligations, so do not include that at the expense of the home lines.

There could be other costs that are from home. Consider by using a record research company to support you in finding out if there are any liens on the business or any back again fees. These could be significant and could include a lot of cash to the price tag on the home. If you know these are heading to be on the business upfront, you won't have to stress about losing hardly any money from them out of your contingency budget.

Mortgage

If you don't have the money to cover your investment properties upfront, you will desire a home loan for the business. If you anticipate paying cash, feel absolve to jump to another section but stay static in this chapter.

The mortgage will cost you big money if you are renovating the business. You will desire a deposit for the home loan. Know how much that is. You could choose to add that either at home cost or in the home loan cost. Each one will continue to work, but beware; this is the only thing that can mix boundaries between your two lines of your financial budget.

Uncover what you'll be paying as an interest. The interest should be computed based on the business price and other things that you use in the mortgage. When you have got a 15-calendar year mortgage, divide the full total interest cost (are available by multiplying the full total interest amount by the interest and subtracting the deposit) by 15. Split it again by 12. That may let you know what the precise interest will be charging you every month. Add that to the range.

If you would prefer to see it altogether, uncover what your mortgage repayment will be every month. It may save some time plus some mathematics to just number this out. Give it its line on your financial budget. Usually, do not put a home loan payment and a pastime repayment in a budget mutually. Choose one or the other. If you are first getting started off with your flipping business, it'll be much easier that you can just see what the actual mortgage loan is when you look at your budget.

Use the builder that you will be using for the next phase. Learn how long she or he thinks the task will take. Inquire further the worst circumstance scenario and become generous if you are figuring it out. For instance, you can include per month or two onto the full total time, so you are completely sure you won't wrap up over budget.

Renovation Costs

Your renovation will be expensive, and will cost you a lot of money. Anticipate paying more than what you intended from the beginning for the reconstruction and ensure that you know what you're getting yourself into. Ask your company to offer the price that he/she will expect the task to cost before you even commence the task on the home. Preferably, you should inquire further before you even choose the business.

Some of the things that you should consider if you are considering the restoration are any structural changes, permit costs and plastic updates of the business. Understand that there can be an inside and outside aspect to every property. You do not want to overlook one or the other because that can have a detrimental influence on the resale of the business.

Your company will let you know what she or he expects you to cover the project. Reserve a bit more than that in your finances, so you have the ability to deal with any surprises that will come up when you are focusing on the project. This will vary with the contingency that the builder has set.

Consider having an inspector go through the home before you get or require the owner to offer an inspection article. This will help you to become more secure in the fact that you will know if the home you are about to flip has more or little structural damage. You should have much problems with the structure of the business particularly if it is an extremely old home. If the business requires a completely new electrical and domestic plumbing system and it includes rotting boards; consider giving it up, you almost certainly don't need that home.

A great company will have a contingency in their restoration budget. That is some money that they can include the price tag on your project that'll be the reserve for the undiscovered. This money can usually be utilized for things that appear during the restoration. Frequently, most businesses tend to hide one big task or several small ones that may arise. If there are extensive problems with the property, you may proceed through your contingency quickly, which may become a huge problem for your financial budget.

Take into account that your restoration budget should be most detrimental case scenario. Develop a collection for the reconstruction on the budget which you have designed for yourself. Ensure that only restoration costs look at these lines, and that you can check it out evidently to see what you will probably purchase with the renovation. This might appear such as a relatively small step, but it could conclude being the most sum of money that you pay throughout the complete project. If you budget correctly, you'll be able to more plainly see if you're getting a package in the business.

Sale Costs

If you haven't ever sold a home before, you may well be surprised to discover that it is not exactly absolved to sell your home. There are a great number of costs that come with the sale of the business.

If you're not a real estate agent or don't have the one which is specifically utilized by your investment property company, you should think about obtaining a real estate certificate. This can help you save plenty of money if you are selling the business and can be worthwhile in the long run. Only think about this if you are truly seriously interested in the investment property business.

The Commission is a very important factor that a lot of people do not consider when they are available to flip their homes. If you are using a Realtor to market your home, you'll be required to pay them a commission payment on the business as sold. Commission rate is some of the deal of the business, usually 10%

or less, and it is how realtors receive a commission. They may have likely done a whole lot of work to help you sell your home, and you will need to think about what the percentage will be if you are considering the budget and set up home as a package.

When you have done any kind of renovation focus on the home, you'll need to have it inspected before you sell it. It's not only the law generally in most areas, but having an inspection survey designed for your audience can help you sell the business more quickly. When you have used an established builder to do the renovations, you should have nothing to stress about as it pertains to your inspection. You would have the ability to stretch your budget if everything was done the proper way.

The very last thing that you'll require to take into account will be the other shutting costs of the business that are unrelated to realtor commission. More often than not, the seller must pay them. Because it is seldom that you can get a buyer who's eager to pay them or even discuss it in an integral part of an offer on the business, you will need to examine these costs if you are looking at the full total price of the business. While shutting costs may seem to be a tiny inconvenience, they can in fact be very costly. Ensure that you know what the common shutting costs would be. Check with your realtor to learn what they'll predict on what you will sell the business for.

Although, it may seem to be a complicated challenging step, it is quite easy. Learn how much the home can cost you for the complete task, how much you'll be spending on the restoration and any deal costs that you will be more likely to incur. Subtract all that by an acceptable comparative price for renovated businesses in the region, and you'll have the quantity that lets you know if you're getting a deal.

Chapter 9: Mortgage Options You Have

For Sale, By Owner

Many individuals who are selling their businesses will offer to finance it for you. Nearly all these folks are those who find themselves looking to get from the owning a home business. You could profit from their losses by purchasing a business from them while not having to offer with traditional mortgage loan terms, but it could be marginally riskier than doing a different type of mortgage. It's important that you work to be sure that you will be getting the most from the mortgage that originates from the owner and that you can learn just as much as you can about the owner before you select one of the mortgage loans or the funding options that exist.

The riskiest part of this type of funding is that you don't have the promises that include the bank mortgage loan. For example, the lender may become more willing to utilize you should something produce the property. There is no guarantee a private seller funding can offer you that kind of leeway.

Through Your Bank

This is exactly what is considered a normal mortgage term. You should be a member of the bank and also have a relationship with your bank if you need to be capable of getting a home loan through it. You must speak to a lender about all the options that exist and ensure that you're getting the best offer possible. That is something that lots of people could find daunting, but it isn't hard if you are in communication with the lender often. The thing that you would like to remember is the fact that the lender is as much as willing to loan you the money (even if he/she does not appear to enjoy it) because that earns profits for the lender (and likely percentage for the individual who's writing the home loan terms).

If you're struggling to get a home loan through the lender when you initially try to get it done, do not quit. The bank will provide you with recommendations on what you must do to enable you get the mortgage loan - follow those ideas! If they request you to fix up your credit, take action. If they request you to bring more income set for a deposit, realize that money. If indeed they tell you that you'll require to repair your bank background, fix it!

The Mortgage for Other Types of Property

There's a chance you will be in a position to get special interest levels on the home loan that you have gotten. The lenders will sometimes have special offers; they could have programs for traders or they could need you to be offering something to all or any of their customers. Regardless the approach you apply in getting the special interest level, do the best you can to enable you get the mortgage.

Even though you can't get a home loan right away, let bank know that you will be considering the special interest. They might be able to store that rate for you and invite you to make use of it down the road. By permitting them to know that you will be thinking about the pace, they will notice that you value the lender and that you will be heading to eventually choose them for the mortgage loan for your investment business. The more traders utilize them for mortgage loans, the more money they will make from the interest levels.

A Loan for Your Business

While you aren't starting a normal kind of business where you will need to provide an office and all the other things that include big businesses, you might still want to get a small business loan to fund everything that you will be doing with you owning a home business. Your loan may well not be adequate to have the ability to pay for the full total price of the business, but it could be enough to truly get you a little part of the home that you would like, so as to start buying things that as to do with real estate.

It is smart to try to obtain the best loan possible. Because the loans are much smaller than the mortgage loans that you'll normally remove for the assistance of shopping for a home, they'll likely have better interest levels that are associated with them. It is smart to try to make certain that you can get a good interest on your loan, although, you may now know that it isn't going for the complete cost of the business that you will be heading to buy.

Using the Calculations

You can certainly find out your mortgage loan amount if you are using a calculator. The solution for understanding your mortgage loan rate is straightforward to follow than the one that requires you doing it the proper way. There are various types of home loans, but if you are using the calculator for some traditional mortgage loans, you will get what you ought to know.

The home loan is your concept times 1 + your interest to the energy of a number of repayments divided by 1 + your interest to the energy of your amount of obligations minus 1.

It will appear to be this; with m = mortgage loan, p = primary, r = interest and n = amount of payments

M = P*r(1+r)^n/(1+4)^n - 1

Chapter 10: Problems that Commercial Property Owners Face

Buying real estate is excellent, and an excellent way to start building the income that will eventually become continual income. It is something that you need to work at than one that should be done with consideration. If you don't learn how to spend money on real business, you will come across even more problems by yourself, and this can be an issue with just how that you do things. It is a good notion to be sure that you can get the most out of you owning a home experience and you know that problems can (and will probably) arise at that time that you will be in business.

You Don't Have the Money

There's always the chance you could go out of money if you are investing. This may happen due to a bad package, because of money that you squandered and even because you didn't do what you had a need to do to have the ability to invest in the proper way. While you go out of capital, you can still do what to help yourself have the investment properties that you'll require.

You may get OPM, credit or other choices that will help you to continue with your investment property. You can also consider borrowing against the business if you are investing so as to continue focusing on it.

Your Market is Bad

It is smart to continue to keep an eyeball on the marketplace in the region that you spend money on. The marketplace is exactly what will determine what you can purchase and what you can sell, nevertheless, you need to be sure that each and every time that you get or sell something, you are carrying on to watch the marketplace. When you initially start, determine just how that the marketplace is going.

If you continue steadily to end up having the market as invested in, you might try to change to rental investment funds or even consider heading to a location that is slightly a long way away from the positioning that you will be presently in - the marketplace will often get far better when you decide to look 40 miles later on to consider properties.

Random Problems that Crop Up

Almost all real estate buyers must encounter circumstances that they didn't see approaching. Whether there's a natural disaster, a difficulty with the home or they unintentionally overpay for something that has been done to the business; you will need to eventually package with something that you didn't expect. Should this happen in early stages in your trading career, you may well not have the funds that you'll require to repair it. If it happens down the road, you often will shell out the dough, but you'll likely be in problem either with money or with time.

Make an effort to keep some cash reserve for these exact things. There is absolutely no way to forecast how much something similar to this will cost you, nevertheless, you can ensure that you're getting the most from it if you wish to have the ability to be secured when it can happens - keeping some money back again can help offset the expenses which come along with problems you weren't planning on. Use this money only for the goal of setting cash back and ensure that you aren't dipping into them for anything apart from an unexpected problem.

Not Making Money

The low sales will most likely eventually occur regardless how good your business is or how hard you work to maintain the best market possible. It is sometimes just completely inescapable to truly have a low sale, and you'll find that you will be having problems maintaining the sales of the businesses that you will be working with. When you have a low sales or something that you weren't looking to happen, you should think about everything that occurs with the businesses.

If you make hardly any money by any means on the business, consider yourself good and chalk it up to bad experience. If it carries on to happen, you might find another market to purchase real property in since it is a recurring problem that is clearly a result of an unhealthy market.

Low sales can often be a very important thing. When you have a home that will not sell for what you would like it to, consider considering other businesses in the same community. The comparative prices will be around exactly like that home, and you'll be in a position to get an improved price on the home or at least have the ability to work out something that is leaner than what you will have paid. Utilize it to your advantage the best way you can as an entrepreneur.

The Wrong Business Type

If you're buying businesses to book for your business, you will sometimes run into bad tenants. These can be people who do not pay their lease, people who eliminate the property and folks who are simply just bad tenants. These can put you back again financially as well as for your investment business generally, but it may be beneficial to try always to undo the harm they have done.

Which means that you will sometimes need to repair up properties, you may want to add additional money to what you earn in the business, and you'll need to screen your tenants better the next time. A very important factor that you should do with your tenants is a background check, a landlord recommendation, and a credit check. Each one of these things can enable you to get tenants that are of an increased quality, and that will help you get the amount of money that you'll require in your pocket. Make sure to always try your very best with your tenants and ensure that you screen them carefully -

unless you feel that they'll be good tenants, simply don't lease to them.

Chapter 11: How to Get the Best Deal on Commercial Property Financing

Financing properties that you will be making the decision to be renting out to businesses are somewhat different than funding homes that you would be renting out. The largest thing is the fact that you cannot have the same kind of loans and incentives for the properties that you will be purchasing to lease to businesses. For example, if you are applying for financing for a home that you will be going to reside in, you will often get an FHA loan that is made for a first-time home buyer. You can even get special rates. You can get this as it pertains to your local rental assets. The properties that you will be going to book shouldn't be purchased with this kind of lending options, and many people won't even speak to you if you haven't done commercial rental buying in the past.

It is a smart decision to ensure that you will always be doing all your best with your rentals investments and that you will be looking for the best funding. Shop around and discover if the financers locally have this kind of options so that you can try with your rentals investment options.

Check the Market Rates

If you're in an awful market for shareholders, you'll be able to find far better rates at your neighborhood banking institutions for the home loan that you will be looking to get. This is due to the fact you'll be able to ensure that you will be getting the best rates since there is not much to choose from locally. Banks will offer you better interest hoping that more buyers comes into play and will desire to be an integral part of your options that are incorporated with your properties. Ensure that you want to do that and you will be in a position to add every one of the things that you'll require to your purchases.

There are often when it could be difficult to find financing if you aren't in a good investment market. Because of this, you might have to go beyond where you live to attempt to find the investment loan rate that you will be looking for. That is more often than not a great option because you will get rates that are competitive and you will be in a position to gain more irrespective of where you live.

If You've Never Bought a Commercial Property ...

While you won't be in a position to get financing as a first-time home buyer, but if you've planned to work with that home as an investment property, you can get good rates over a fire time entrepreneur loan. That is something that banking institutions can do to encourage visitors to have the ability to come for you and discover what you are doing with the lending options that exist locally. It's important to note that you'll need to make certain that you meet all the requirements. The bankers frequently have very rigid options so that you can figure out what you are also doing to decide the sort of first-time investment that will continue to work best with your alternatives.

There are various things that you need to satisfy. For instance, you need to make certain that you will be going to be capable of getting all the options that you'll require with your investment. You need to have a whole lot of various things that will show that you will be going to be always a great investor. Finance institutions won't want you if indeed they feel that you will choose a property and then will be unsuccessful with your investment because you don't know what you do. While they recognize that first-time buyers can be high-risk, they need you showing them that you will be the cheapest risk of every one of the investors they have talked with.

Special Offers for Members of the Bank

You will more often than not get an improved interest at a loan provider that you will be an associate of. This is the first place that you should check to determine which kind of mortgage interest they offer. There's a chance that the member mortgage loan price will be even significantly less than the price tag on what you will pay for another kind of investment loan. Keep this at heart if you are shopping for lending options to have the ability of funding your investment property.

The probabilities are that you have got a bank-account with a checking or a checking account at the lender that you will be an associate of. If you've ever noticed, they are doing more than the easy banking that you'll require. Even though you have a home loan with a particular lender for your home, you might talk with them first as it pertains to the mortgage loans on your initial investment properties. The probabilities are that you can get an extremely great rate on loan for this property.

Sites that Are Historical

These kinds of loans will be the best ones. They may have low interest, are easy to acquire and will make you able to maximize the sum of money from the properties that you have got. It's important that you look for this if you want to go into a historical home.

There are vary types of historical buildings and lending options that go with them, so, ensure that you know what you are interested in. It could be complicated to determine precisely what the lender wants someone to fulfill, so, be certain that you will always be looking to make certain that you will be getting the most with it. There are various options for your mortgage loan, which is essential that you try to be sure that you will be getting the best package possible.

Chapter 12: The Plan for Your Property Investment Business

Any business proprietor, whatever business they can be in, will let you know that you'll require to truly have a business plan before you even think about starting your business. You intend to be in the business enterprise of real business investing, and which means that you'll have your own business. To be certain that it's going to achieve success and become everything that you would like it to be, you will need to ensure that you will be attempting to get the most out of business. Using this method, you will place yourself up to get various goals, which can make it easier so that you can strike the goals.

Decide on the Goals for Your Plan

You ought to have specific goals for what you would like regarding your real property making an investment business. These can be anything from a number of businesses that you would like to possess to the money that you would like to make in 12 months. Use both short-term and permanent goals to be capable of getting the most information on your business plan.

Short-term goals include:

- Buy a business
- Sell a business

- Convert your first profit

Long run goals include:

- Making your first $100,000

- Buying a major property

- Extending your business

- Retiring successfully

It's important to acquire both permanent and short-term goals, nevertheless, you should ensure that your short-term goals are always working toward your long-term goals to enable you to eventually reach them even if it's years from now.

Before you do other things, jot down five short-term goals and five long-term goals that you would like to perform for your real estate industry.

Everything in the program

Things that you'll need to acquire in your business plan are:

- Goals - adding these first will point out to you why you performed this to begin with

- Mission assertion - this is exactly what will let you know why you do what you do with your owning a home business

- Money - you understand where your cash reaches today and exactly how much you have; but what you do not know is where your cash is likely to be at. Keep an eye on this and keep it in another location of your business plan. Compare the amount of money that you really wish to acquire to the money that you now have. This will not only give you a motivation always to keep working for more, but it will also show you what lengths you attended when you do learn to see a great deal of success.

- Strategy - jot down the way that you will be going to generate profits and stay with it so you will have the ability to ensure that you will be buying the correct way

- Requirements - keep an eye on what you would like to do and just how that you would like to invest. Jot down which kind of properties you will buy and keep a set of "hard forward" properties that you'll never buy. This will help you keep your eyesight in mind in case you feel just like something is an extremely good deal.

- Time shape - when would you like to have ten properties, be wealthy, retire, etc.? Write it down.

- Market - accumulate every one of the information you know about your market. When you yourself have on paper everything you know about the marketplace that you will be an integral part of, venture out and find out more information about any of it. Keep all that in your business plan, and in case something changes on the market, change it out in your business plan too

-       Plan for advertising - you have to market your owning a home business for some reasons, and also keep an eye on how you will be able to get it done when you yourself have started the business enterprise. It's important you know in advance how you will market your business so you don't need to get worried about taking extra steps when it's time to advertise yourself

-       Make examples - come on world home elevators which kind of offers you different properties locally. Write them down and then make a pretend package with them. Keep this in your business plan so as to have an opportunity to consider it. Be realistic about any of it to enable you to come back and strategies with it down the road.

Taking Actionable Steps

There is absolutely no reason to truly have a business plan if you aren't in a position to put it into action. Begin working on your business plan once you recognize that is something that you would like to do. When you're able to create the business enterprise plan, you already are taking action, and you'll be able to set into play once you are prepared to start. As your business plan includes everything about how precisely you're going to begin buying a real estate, just do it. The earlier you begin, the sooner you'll be able to earn a living.

Trying New Changes

There's always an opportunity that your plan could change. You might see more opportunities someplace else, or you might get one of these different kinds of real estate making an investment. No matter what changes you make to your owning a home business, ensure that you do it in a manner that will help you to revise your business plan and make sure it corresponds with your initial business plan. If you're going to have to put more info into the business, you should keep the business plan modified, and you ought to ensure that you do it to your very best capabilities, so you need not worry about different techniques that will fit into the program. Make an effort to always upgrade your plan in your business once you know that there surely is going to be always a major change in the manner you run the business enterprise.

Chapter 13: Terms that You Will Find in Commercial Real Estate

Commercial property – any property that people cannot live in; it could be offices, a simple warehouse building or anything else where business is conducted; almost all commercial buildings are not zoned for people to live in

Real estate – anything that you can own that is a property or related to a property; a piece of land is real estate, a home is real estate, a vehicle is not real estate (but is an investment)

Lessor - the individual who is hiring out the business; also, sometimes known as a landlord in residential property management

Lessee - the individual or individuals who is renting the business; also, sometimes known as the renter or the renter of the business

Yield - the speed that you earn things with your ventures

Insurance - an insurance plan that is bought that will protect the business or the business from certain issues that are out of the hands

Homeowner - the individual who owns the business; the name that the deed is within

Zoning - this is exactly what determines whether you could have a home in a commercial area or perhaps a commercial business in a home area; you will need to ensure that you will be within certain requirements for the zoning in your township or your unique area

Revenues - the money that someone makes per month before fees; often about 30% greater than the real money that the individual brings home

Return - the money that you will get back again from something you have put back to it

Payment - the money that you pay to the lender or the mortgagor frequently

Ordinances - guidelines that dictate just how you do things from; if you desire a building permit aside of the road that you will be permitted to put your garbage can on

Notice - an offer that was written and has newspaper proof; holding frequently used before mortgages

HELOC - also known as a home collateral credit line; money that is lent against the total amount that you have got in equity at home

Ground rent - when someone rents a bit of land; normal with trailer renting as well as in traditional types of truck parks

Grantor - the individual or the people who provides deed

General builder - the individual or company that develops buildings or does renovations on a business; is certified to take action

Net price - the quantity that you will be worth as it pertains to the properties that you possess and things that you do

Multi-dwelling - another name for a flat organic - has many items but only 1 home loan to it

Capital - the money that is available for you; income as well as debts which you can use in your favor

Beneficiary - the individual who receives the amount of money from the investment

Bankruptcy – the way that financial responsibilities are released from your business; you will use this in extreme circumstances and, hopefully, you will never need to use it

As-is - no promises on the business or the building; you will generally come across this when you are buying a property; but you should never try to rent out a property on an as-is basis because it could cause major problems

Home loan - the paperwork that presents that you will be in charge of your payment; this can be a lien or a loan company or other entity places against the business that you possess

Default - a whole incapability to meet obligations

Deed - the file that presents who owns the property is really as well as who owns the property has been in the past

Commercial property real business investing - Extra cash with the expectations to getting a go back on the amount of money you have allocated to a property

Chapter 14: The Right Commercial Property for You

There are very a few factors that get into deciding which property will work out for you. You will need to ensure that you have the ability to maximize sum of money possible, and that you will be heading to get just what you will need with your premises. The largest problem with not deciding on the best property is that you'll hardly make any money. Things that you need to think through when you find a business are:

The Cost

The main thing that you'll check out is the price tag on the property. Your cost should be considerably below what your 10-season projection is on the business that you will be heading to be booking out. To find this out, you will need to choose how much you will rent the business out for each and every month and multiple it by 120 (for the 120 weeks of another 10 years).

If you're in a position to have an increased amount over that time frame, you'll be able to get the best options possible as it pertains to your cost of the business.

Is Your Business Worth It?

You'll also need to take the worthiness of the business under consideration. While this will not determine what you'll be paying for the business every time that you make the mortgage repayment, it can help you if you want to borrow against the business or something similar. There are various things that go into the value of the properties that you will be considering, so make certain you have a professional who can let you know what the worthiness of the business is.

Because you feel that a property will probably be worth something doesn't imply that it really is. Only a specialist can let you know what the business is worth with regards to the age of the business, just how that it's been looked after and other activities that go into the consideration of the worthiness of the business. Make sure to always know this before you even make an effort to negotiate on the price tag on the home so you will not conclude losing profits on a business that's not quite what you thought it might be worth.

What is Your Market?

With regards to the area that you will be in, your premises will be worthwhile different amounts. The marketplace that you will be in will determine the quantity of the business value and what you would be capable of getting for this when you hire it out. It will determine what you will need to pay for the business.

If you're going to make certain that you will be getting the largest value for the rentals investment that you will be looking at, you'll need to learn your market. Knowing the marketplace is nearly as important as knowing the expense of the home, the worthiness of the business and the rest that switches into the process.

To determine which kind of market you are in, you should think about the several properties locally. Compare these to the overall economy of where you are and ensure that you know the proper way to figure out things that you will be doing with the business. It's also advisable to find out if more folks locally lease or if more folks own. This can make an enormous difference in what you ought to be spending money on the property.

Making That Payment

Unless you are paying cash for your rentals investment, you will need to know what your mortgage repayment will end up like. This is found easily by heading to the lender what your location is going to obtain the mortgage loan from and learning what it'll be like. You do not necessarily need to have a home in your places to determine what the mortgage loan will end up like, but you'll need to make certain that you will be figuring out the proper way to purchase that. There are various options as it pertains to your home loan, so ensure that you really know what type you have, the total amount that you will probably pay and any extra things you will be spending money on with the home loan that you have developed.

If you wish to maximize sum of money possible, you should be prepared to rent the business out for just two times the home loan amount monthly. Which means that you'll be able to make two times obligations, and pay the home loan off faster than have total income by the end of the mortgage loan or that you can merely use the income of the business to live from every month (this is actually the option that almost all of men and women choose).

Can You Rent it Out?

The possibility of booking a home is something that you'll require to determine if you are taking a look at the rentals investment properties. If you're unable to rent the business out, you won't have the ability to earn a living from it. A couple of things that you should consider if you are planning on booking out a home:

- Is there a higher demand for renting locally?
- What kind of businesses are people looking for?

- Will your lease be very costly?

Each one of these things will determine if you will in actuality have the ability to rent the business out. If you discover that you will be unable to find out the answers to them, the probabilities are that the business will not book easily and you'll be caught up with an investment property that's not heading to make hardly any money for you. You may want to consider different kinds of businesses to book with in regards to the area that you will be in.

Chapter 15: Leaving the Real Estate Game

If you are first engaging in commercial property real business investing, you almost certainly are not taking into consideration the long haul (or possibly you are in which particular case - go you!). The proper thing to do is to consider your time of retirement from the start of your adventure into the commercial property real business investment. Some individuals start out at this business in the later part of their lives, which is okay. Nevertheless, you should work out how you will escape it sooner or later to enable you to truly be retired rather than just enjoying the unaggressive income.

The Exact Time

There is absolutely no right time that is wonderful for everyone. Generally, you'll be ready to leave from the commercial property investment game when you are feeling that you have got developed enough capital to go on for the others you will ever have. Until then, you can merely just keep collecting on the businesses since it is truly unaggressive income you don't want to do much for. Even though you are controlling your own properties, it continues to be essential that you try to be sure that you will be doing everything the correct way and that you will be getting truly the most from the properties that you will be profiting from.

Don't take action until it seems best for the investment that you have made.

No Debt with Property

In most cases, your investment properties should be paid prior to deciding to leave the commercial property investment game. That is true for some cases but might not exactly continually be true if you have very significant home loans. For instance, you may well not have the ability to pay back a multimillion buck complex; nevertheless, you should ensure that most of it is paid for or that you will not be ugly on the home loan before you decide to market it and leave the commercial property real property game.

You should do your very best as it pertains to paying down your rental investment funds. Whether which means that you will be heading to make dual payments, you will add different alternatives to the businesses or you will be in a position to put more income into them than what you'd actually planned. Paying down your investment properties is the ultimate way to make the largest profit possible from your investment.

Change the Way It is Handled

Before you decide to leave the commercial property investment industry, you should attempt to transfer a lot of the duties to a management team. There are several property management companies that'll be able to handle most big things that continue with your property. When you must purchase them, it'll be worth it; so that you can ensure that you're getting the truly best experience. All you have to do is relax and make an effort to pay for things that the company does. They will cope with the rest from it for you, so you don't need to worry regarding it.

A management company can show you the several techniques commercial property real business works and just how that you can continue earning money even once you've stepped back again from the investment. The management company will also make it easier so that you can decide on what you will do with the business when you finally make a decision to quit the commercial property investment. Always try to be sure that you will be adding various things to your investment and that you will be always seeing your management team.

Sold for Total Profit

The end game of any commercial property real estate investor is to market their investment property for a complete profit. There are factors to consider if you are to make certain that you will be getting the most from the process, and that you truly sell it for what it probably worth. A very important factor that you should be shopping for is the costs of businesses to increase from the stage where these were at. It really is smart to try and ensure that you're getting the best opportunity possible.

There are multiple reasons that you might desire to be in a position to get the most sum of money from your options. It is smart to try to sell your premises to discover the best profit possible. The business should prepare you to sell and really should be an easy one that you can make a good choice with. It'll allow you the opportunity to truly add value to your riches that you have previously created on the total amount that you placed into the property.

Spending Capital You Made with Commercial Property

Once you've sold your premises, try to understand that the riches that you earn from it is exactly what you will have to count on for a long period. Although it may appear such as a large amount of money, it will have to go on you for some time, particularly if you are retired from other things that you performed. Usually, do not spend every one of the money at one time. It is always advisable not to spend it extravagantly. It really is smart to act like you do not have the amount of money until you need it to enable you to avoid any issues that will come up with the amount of money that you earn - you ought to be careful to keep that money and ensure that you aren't spending an excessive amount of it to the stage where you do not have any left.

If your online worth has ended one million us dollars, it may be beneficial to have a person who will help you with riches management. It is because it could be hard to take care of all your own money if you aren't familiar with having that amount. Make sure that you always make an effort to manage the amount of money in the simplest way possible.

Conclusion

Thanks for making it through to the end of *Commercial Real Estate Guide*. Let's hope it was informative and able to provide you with all of the tools you need to achieve your goals of achieving success in the commercial real estate business.

The next step is to start looking for commercial properties in your area and figure out what is going to work best for you. Have a good understanding of what is going to work and what will not work in the area that you are in so that you can make sure that you are not losing out on the various income opportunities of properties. There are many options that you can choose from; so, make sure that you are choosing the correct commercial real estate. You can benefit and make the most amount of money when you know what you want and you go for it.

Finally, if you found this book useful in any way, a review on Amazon is always appreciated!

Made in the USA
Lexington, KY
09 November 2017